Sea Stars
and
Dragons

Sea Stars
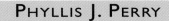
and
Dragons

PHYLLIS J. PERRY

A First Book

Franklin Watts

A Division of Grolier Publishing

New York   London   Hong Kong   Sydney

Danbury, Connecticut

Cover and Interior Design by Molly Heron
Cover photographs copyright ©: **Kjell B. Sandved; Visuals Unlimited (inset).**
Photographs copyright ©: Visuals Unlimited: pp. 8 (Michael G. Gabridge), 16
(Richard Thom), 29 (Patrice), 31, 33, 42, (all Dave B. Fleetham), 34, 43 (both Glenn
M. Oliver), 36 (Richard L. Carlton), 38 (William Jorgensen),40 (Daniel W.
Gotshall), 47 (Triarch), 48 (A.D. Copley), 50 (Bruce Cushing), 56 (Kjell B. Sandved),
57 (W. Ober); The Wildlife Collection: pp. 11, 15, 24 (all Dean Lee), 23, 45, 53, 54
(all Chris Huss); Animals Animals: pp. 12 (W. Gregory Brown), 19, 20 (both Rudie
Kuiter); Kjell B. Sandved: p. 27

Library of Congress Cataloging-in-Publication Data

Perry, Phyllis Jean.
Sea stars and dragons / by Phyllis J. Perry.
p. cm. — (A First book)
Includes bibliographical references and index.
Summary: Describes the physical characteristics and behaviors
of sea stars and sea horses.
ISBN 0-531-20223-2
1. Starfishes—Juvenile literature. 2. Sea horses—Juvenile literature. [1. Sea
horses. 2. Marine animals.]
I. Title. QL384.A8P47 1996
593.9'3—dc20
341.23—dc20   95-11292   CIP AC

Library of Congress Cataloging-in-Publication Data
Copyright © 1996 by Phyllis J. Perry
Printed in the United States of America
6 5 4 3 2 1

 *For*

DAVID,
WHO HAS ALWAYS BEEN A SAILOR AT HEART;

JANET,
WHOSE AQUARIA ARE OBJECTS OF BEAUTY;
AND

JILL,
WHO LOVES THE SEA.

Contents

These stars live in the sea.

≈ I ≈

A Fairyland Under the Sea

Do you believe in dragons? Are there stars in the sea? Wait! Before you smile and shake your head "no," you had better read on a little further. You see, this book is all about stars and dragons. It is not about the stars you see shining on a dark night, but real live sea stars. And it is not about the pretend fire-breathing dragons of fairy tales, but real live sea dragons.

All kinds of animals in every shape, size, and color you can imagine live in the sea. The huge whale, the frightening shark, and the tiny shrimp live there. Many exotic animals do too, including the sea cow, sea elephant, and sea cucumber.

Water covers about two-thirds of our earth's surface. There is room in the great oceans and seas for billions of living things. There are *corals* shaped like castles and *anemones* waving delicate branches resembling flowers. They make the underwater world look like a fairyland. So perhaps we shouldn't be surprised to learn that stars and dragons live in the sea too. And they do.

Sea stars and sea dragons are not related to each other, but they do have some enchanting characteristics in common. Each of these creatures does many strange and wonderful things that are sure to astonish you. Get ready to take a fantastic voyage into the land of sea stars and dragons.

This is not a make-believe dragon, but a real live sea horse called the Australian sea dragon.

2

Dragons of the Sea

One of the most interesting animals of all in the sea looks a lot like a little dragon or a tiny horse. You probably know this creature best by the name sea horse.

There are many different kinds of sea horses. The pygmy sea horse is one of the smallest. It is only 1 or 2 inches (3 to 5 cm) long when fully grown, at about the age of only three months. Even the biggest of sea horses measures not much over 1 foot (30 cm) long.

This sea horse lives in the Caribbean Sea.

These little sea dragons are too small to be very frightening, but they certainly are fascinating.

If you ever see a live sea horse, one of the first things you might notice is its tail. It is long and curls up at the tip. Like a monkey's tail, the sea horse's tail can act as a convenient anchor. The tip of the tail curls and holds onto things.

The sea horse may curl the tip of its tail around a piece of seaweed or coral, for instance. This prevents it from being washed away by waves or currents. Anchored, it can remain still and hidden from many other sea animals that would like to eat it. Sometimes the sea horse hangs on for hours, blending in with eelgrass and sea whips, a kind of coral.

Some sea horses have something else that helps *camouflage* them. They have *cirri*, which are like whiskers. The cirri look like bits of seaweed stuck to the sea horse, so they help it blend in with seaweed.

The sea horse can coil its tail into a tight spiral by curling it forward, or it can straighten it out completely. But it cannot curl its tail backward. It can

Sea horses curl their tails around plants to hold on.

The sea horse has two earlike fins and a large fin on its back.
It has gills in front of the earlike fins.

hold onto things only when the tail is coiled forward. Even though they are tiny, baby sea horses also coil their tails and cling to thin reeds.

A sea horse is not covered in scales as most fish are. Bony plates and spikes called *spines* cover the skin of the sea horse. These protect it like armor.

The sea horse has transparent fins that are fan-shaped. The two earlike fins on the head make the sea horse look like a tiny horse or a dragon. They help maintain its position in the water. Amazingly enough, if a sea horse loses a fin in an accident, it can grow a new one in about two weeks. This seemingly magical ability is called *regeneration*.

If you saw a sea horse, you couldn't help noticing its eyes. In baby sea horses, they seem particularly big. These eyes are special, because the adult sea horse can move one eye while keeping the other eye quite still! The sea horse may look ahead with one eye, and at the same time look down or up or behind with the other eye.

Since it can look in two directions at once, it is not easy for another creature to come along unnoticed and surprise the little sea dragon. Not only can a sea horse spot an enemy coming, but it can also easily spy any food that is nearby.

THE PREGNANT FATHER

You might think a sea creature that looks like a miniature dragon and has a tail like a monkey's is strange enough. But that's not all that is unusual about sea horses. One of the oddest things about them is the way baby sea horses are born. The mother lays the eggs, but it is the father who gives birth.

The mother sea horse puts her eggs in the *brood pouch* of the father. This brood pouch is on the front of the male sea horse, just above his tail. Perhaps it will remind you a little of the pocket on a kangaroo. The father baby-sits, keeping the eggs safely in his pouch until they are ready to hatch. His pouch, filled with all those eggs, makes the father sea horse look fat.

Some sea horse eggs hatch in about ten days, while other kinds of sea horse eggs take as long as forty-five days. Even after the eggs have finally hatched, the worries of the father sea horse are not yet over.

Sometimes the father sea horse has a hard time getting all of the newly hatched babies out of his pouch. In trying to expel them, the sea horse contracts his body and rubs the pouch against something hard, like a piece of coral, until there is an opening through which the babies can come out.

Only a few sea horses come out at a time, but the father sea horse keeps rubbing away at his pouch until he pops all the babies out. There may be 150 to 200 babies in a brood.

When the baby sea horses are first born, they are less than 1/2 inch (1 cm) in size. Their bodies are so clear that you can see right through them. But in a few days, they develop color. Sea horses are gray, black, red, yel-

A mother sea horse deposits her eggs in a father sea horse's belly.

A father sea horse expels newly hatched babies from an opening in his stomach.

low, green, white, and even silver. They can be very beautiful.

As soon as they hatch, these tiny animals are on their own. Unlike baby birds, no mother or father carries tasty food to them in a nest. Unlike kittens or puppies, they cannot cuddle close to their mothers to nurse. But little sea horses can swim, and they must quickly swim away and find their own food.

Baby sea horses need to hide so that they won't be eaten. As they conceal themselves among the seaweed and coral, they spend much of their time eating because they are very hungry.

At first the baby sea horse swims like most other fish, with its head in front and tail floating out behind. Then in a few days, the sea horse does a funny thing. It slowly bends so that it is upright in the water, holding its head up and its tail down. Now it truly looks like a little dragon or horse gently galloping through the sea.

The sea horse is often simply carried along by currents in the water. But it can also swim slowly in its upright position, moving itself weakly with its back fin, or *dorsal fin*.

When the sea horse wants to move forward or backward, it vibrates the dorsal fin rapidly from side to side. To go up or down, it ripples the dorsal fin lengthwise. When it is swimming along quite leisurely, fluttering its fins, the sea horse looks as if it is fanning itself.

Sea horses have *gills* that take oxygen from the water. The gills are located above the breast fins and are protected with gill covers. The sea horse takes a mouthful of water and passes it through the gills. They take in the oxygen, and the water flows out from under the gill covers.

A BUILT-IN STRAW

Since you've already learned that this little animal has a tail like a monkey's, and a pouch like a kangaroo's, it may not surprise you to learn that sea horses eat in a most peculiar fashion. It is something like the way you sip a milk shake through a straw.

At the end of its tubelike snout, the sea horse has a tiny mouth with no teeth. Through the tube, the sea horse can quickly suck in food that comes near it.

Sea horses eat all kinds of tiny animals such as small shrimp, other crustaceans, baby fish, and different kinds of larvae. By sucking through its tube, the little sea dragon takes in a large amount of food. Would you believe that a sea horse may eat for as long as ten hours a day? Now that's a lot of eating! In that time, the sea horse may eat over three thousand tiny shrimp.

A sea horse's snout sucks in food like a straw.

22

The Magic of Sea Horses

Sea dragons, or sea horses, are found in saltwaters all over the world. They live on both coasts of South America, in the Gulf of Mexico, near the continent of Australia, on the Atlantic coasts of Europe and Africa, in the Indo-Pacific, and on both coasts of the United States. Sea horses live in shallow water among the seaweed, in coral reefs, and in marine grasses.

Of all the sea horses, the Australian sea dragon is perhaps the most spectacular. This queer creature

The Australian sea dragon blends in especially well with plants. Notice its large earlike fins.

looks more like a plant than an animal. Sticking out all over its body are little pieces that look like leaves and branches. Its camouflage is so good that when it hides among rockweed, it is almost impossible to see.

The Australian sea dragon holds onto the rockweed with its special coiled tail and floats along with the plants. Since it has no way to protect itself from hungry fish that might eat it, this sea dragon depends on its ability to hide from them.

Because they look so interesting, sea horses have been used by people in many unusual ways. In the game of chess, one of the pieces, called the knight, is shaped like a horse. These playing pieces are usually carved from wood or stone, but some have been made from dead sea horses that have been preserved and mounted.

When dead sea horses are dried and coated, they are used for many other kinds of decorations. Sometimes they are coated in clear plastic and sold as paper weights or pen holders for desks. Often they are sold in shops along with pieces of coral and seashells.

In the past, some people thought that the sea horse was magical and could cure many ills. In China long ago, the sea horse was ground up into a kind of powder that was used in making many different medicines. In Italy, people wore sea horses as good luck charms. The little sea dragon was even carved on an ancient mummy case found in Egypt. So we know that people all over

Sea horse skeletons are still sold as medicine in Hong Kong.

the world have been interested in this little dragon of the deep for a long, long time.

It is possible to keep live sea horses in a *marine* aquarium. This kind of aquarium is different from the aquariums of goldfish or tropical fish that most people have, because it contains saltwater instead of fresh water. It is not easy to keep a sea horse healthy in an aquarium, but it can be done.

The favorite for aquariums is the pygmy sea horse, which is found in the waters near Florida and the Gulf of Mexico. To set up a home for a pair of pygmy sea horses, you should use a 2- or 3-gallon (7- or 11-liter) aquarium.

You also need an air pump and filter to keep the water in good condition. The temperature of the water should not be allowed to go below 65 degrees F (18 degrees C).

A hydrometer is needed to ensure that the water is not too salty. It should not rise above a reading of 1.025. The sea horses need live food such as brine shrimp, which you can either purchase or easily raise yourself.

Scientists guess that in its natural habitat a sea horse normally lives from two to six years. But in an aquarium, pygmy sea horses may live for less than a year and larger sea horses may live for about a year and a half. The larger kinds of sea horses are hard to keep in aquariums because their young tend to get many diseases.

People who keep sea horses alive in aquariums can watch the eggs being laid and the baby sea horses hatching. Pygmy sea horses lay about twenty-five eggs as often as twice a month. The eggs hatch in about ten days.

The pygmy sea horse is sometimes kept in
marine aquariums.

The larger Atlantic sea horse, which may lay up to two hundred eggs at a time, does not hatch from the egg for about forty-five days. The baby Atlantic sea horse is fully grown when it is about ten months old, and it is then usually about 5 inches (13 cm) long.

Two kinds of Mediterranean sea horses have been kept alive successfully in aquariums, and these sea horses also lay about two hundred eggs at a time.

BUT IS IT A FISH?

Now that you have had a good look at the sea horse or dragon, you may well wonder whether or not it is really a fish at all. There are many different kinds of fish, and they certainly do not all look alike, but the sea horse is very strange-looking indeed.

How can you tell if the sea horse really is a fish? To be a true fish, an animal must have a backbone, fins, gills, and must never grow arms or legs. If you remember those few things, you have a simple test for separating true fish from other animals that live in or near the water.

Think about this test, and then try to apply it. Although it has great size, at first glance the whale really looks more like a fish than does a little sea horse. The whale has a sleek body and a fishy-looking tail.

However, whales do not have gills; they have lungs, just as people do, for breathing in air. A whale must come up to the surface of the ocean to breathe air.

This pipefish is a relative of sea horses that swims like a fish.

Since it doesn't have gills, you know that the whale is not a fish.

Although a fully grown frog does not look at all like a fish, a frog does go through a stage when, as a tadpole, it looks much like a fish. As the tadpole develops, it grows legs. Since animals that grow arms or legs are not fish, you know that the tadpole cannot be a fish.

Even though the jellyfish has the word "fish" in its name, it is not a true fish either. The sea jelly does not have a backbone, and it does not have gills or fins. It cannot pass your test for being a fish.

Now look carefully at the sea horse or sea dragon. Although it is surely an unusual little creature, the sea horse does have a backbone, gills, fins, and never grows arms or legs. It passes your test, so you know that the sea horse is a fish after all.

The sea horse is a member of the strange family of fishes called the pipefishes. A pipefish, with a body that looks like a pipe or pencil, grows to be about 18 inches (46 cm) long. All the members of this family have a tiny mouth at the end of a tubelike snout. They all have large eyes, a short fin close to the middle of their back, and long, narrow tails.

Pipefishes have both an internal skeleton and an external skeleton. The external skeleton has bony plates connected by rings. The strange-looking trumpetfish and cornetfish are also distant relatives of the sea horse.

The trumpetfish is a pipefish distantly related to the sea horse.

A FAIRYTALE COME TRUE

Except in storybooks, you can never hope to meet a gigantic fire-breathing dragon, but you may be lucky enough to one day see a live little dragon of the deep, a sea horse. If you do, you will meet one of the most interesting fish in all the sea.

A yellow cushion star rests among blood stars.

≈ 4 ≈

The Stars of the Sea

✦

*I*f you think sea dragons seem like magical creatures, wait until you learn about sea stars. Sea stars used to be called starfish, but a sea star is not a fish at all.

Remember your test for a true fish? A true fish never grows arms or legs. Sea stars have arms called *rays*. Sea stars belong to a special group of animals known as the spiny-skinned animals. The name comes from the spines that stick out from their bodies.

There are about 1,600 known kinds of sea stars. They are found in all the oceans of the world. Some even live in the Arctic and Antarctica. Sea stars can live only in saltwater. Many species can be found along the tide line of the sea shore on both the Atlantic and

The common sea star has sharp, bony spines covering its body.

Pacific coasts of the United States. Others live many thousands of feet down at the bottom of the sea.

As adults, sea stars may measure as little as 1/2 inch (1 cm) across and as large as almost 3 feet (90 cm) across. Common colors for sea stars are yellow, orange, pink, red, green, purple, blue, and gray.

Like other animals, there are certain things a sea star needs to stay alive. It must have food. It must have oxygen. A sea star must be in saltwater, and it must protect itself from being eaten. To stay alive, the sea star uses its special body.

Perhaps the best way to learn about sea stars is to study one kind very carefully. What you learn about it will help you understand other sea stars, too. Let's look at what is often called the common sea star.

The common sea star may be brown, bronze, orange, or even purple or green. When it is fully grown, this animal will measure between 6 and 11 inches (15 and 28 cm) from the tip of one arm, or ray, across to the tip of another.

Like all sea stars, the common sea star has no head. Instead, it has a flat disk in the center of its body that blends into its five arms, or rays. The body of a sea star is protected by a kind of skeleton—the many small, sharp spines covering its body. Among the spines are tiny pincers that can clamp onto rocks or food.

Growing up out of the thin covering on top of the sea star body are hundreds of tiny bumps that look something like little fingers. These are the gills of the sea star. The gills are hollow. They have thin walls and open into the body of the sea star.

Fresh seawater around the sea star comes in through the gills, which transfer oxygen from the water into the body fluid of the sea star. The water that is drawn in through the openings then travels through canals along the outside of the body to the arms. The arms send the water to little tube feet on the underside of the body, where the water exits. The sea star can move its feet by pumping water into them.

If a fish should bump against the sea star, the pincers will rise. They wave about and snap. If they touch the fish, they will pinch tightly and will not let go. Hundreds of these little pincers can hold a small crab or fish until the sea star decides to eat, or until the fish or crab dies.

The top side of the common sea star has gills and tiny pincers in the center.

Pincers also help to keep the arms of the sea star clean. When bits of sand, seaweed, or sea animals collect between the spines of the sea star, the pincers pick up the litter and drop it back into the sea.

A large crab or fish may attack a sea star and tear off a number of the little pincers, or even an arm. But that does not really bother the sea star. One of the most wondrous things about a sea star is that it can grow back a piece of its body that is torn away. Like the sea horse, it has the ability to regenerate.

The sea horse, you may recall, can grow back a fin if it loses one. Unfortunately, it cannot regrow any other part of its body. But even if a sea star loses one of its arms, it will grow a new one to replace it. So if you should see a sea star with four arms and a bump where the fifth arm should be, you can be sure the missing arm will soon grow back.

Sea stars are eaten by fish, crabs, and other sea stars, but their greatest enemies are gulls and shore birds.

FEASTING ON SHELLFISH

To understand how the sea star gets its food, you need to know more about its arms. The underside of the arm of a sea star is complicated. There are usually two or four rows of hundreds of tiny tube feet that run down the center of the arm, or ray, in a little groove. They are part of the sea star's canal system.

Each tube foot ends in a sucking disk. These suckers let the sea star cling to a rock or climb a steep surface such as the side of an underwater cave.

Because of the loose kind of skeleton it has, the arms of the sea star bend easily. Sometimes they bend toward the shell of a *mussel* so that the suckers can attach to it. Then the center of the sea star rises. More suckers on another arm attach to the mussel. Each arm grips one of the mussel's two valves, the openings to the soft part of the mussel. The sea star pulls while the mussel tries to keep its valves tightly closed.

When the mussel tires and opens a little, the sea star flattens down over its food. What happens next is truly amazing. The sea star has a mouth on the underside of its body, but it does not pull its food into its mouth as we do. Instead, it pushes part of its stomach out through the mouth and onto the food!

The stomach of the sea star begins to digest the food using a yellowish fluid. After the soft parts of the mussel are digested, the empty shell is released. It may take several hours for a sea star to finish its meal.

This fragile star is regenerating two rays that were torn off.

Sea stars have tube feet underneath each ray.

This sea star is eating a clam by pushing its stomach, on the center of its underside, in between the clamshells.

Some kinds of sea stars like to eat a lot of oysters. A sea star is able to partially pull open an oyster by using the suckers on its arms. Some scientists believe that the sea star also puts out a kind of poison to weaken the oyster. Once the oyster shell is partly opened, the sea star squeezes a part of its stomach into the opening between the shells and begins to digest the oyster. The stomach can move through a crack less than 1 mm (1/25 inch) wide.

As the oyster shell opens wider, the sea star can put more of its stomach inside. When it has finished eating, the sea star leaves an empty oyster shell. Because they eat so many oysters, sea stars are a big problem for oyster fishermen.

Another food that some sea stars like to eat is the *scallop*. Often, however, scallops can escape from sea stars. A scallop has two rows of bright blue eyes. When it sees the sea star coming its way, the scallop can shoot off for a short distance like a little jet. The sea star does not have eyes, but it does have eyespots at the ends of its arms. These eyespots can sense light and dark.

Sea stars get around by walking along rocks or the bottom. When a sea star walks, one arm, the "head arm," leads the way. The tube feet of the head arm extend, and the suckers stick to a rock. Then the other four arms move close to the head arm, and the suckers on these tube feet stick also. The head arm stretches out again in the direction the sea star wants to go, and takes another grip.

A sea star does not move very quickly. It can go about 6 inches (15 cm) in a minute. The tube feet of a sea star can hold very tightly to a rock. Even a pull of

The tube feet of the sea star have a powerful grip.

one hundred pounds sometimes cannot loosen a sea star that is gripping tightly.

The sea star has feet on only one side of its body—the underside. When a sea star is turned over on its back, it must right itself. One, two, or three arms curve under so that the tube feet can grip the bottom. These arms then flip the sea star over in a kind of somersault.

SPAWNING PARTY

If you saw a baby sea star, you might not know what it was. It does not look at all like a grown sea star. It looks more like a blob of jelly.

Sea stars *spawn*, or make babies, together in a group all at once. And they don't even have to touch one another when they do it. The male and female sea stars cast thousands of eggs and sperm into the sea. Eggs and sperm unite and develop into small larvae that float in the water.

After the baby sea stars hatch from the larvae, they swim about. The baby swims by using little hairs near its mouth to propel it.

Little sea stars live on *plankton*, microscopic plants and animals in the water. When baby sea stars are between two and eight weeks old, they sink to the bottom and begin to grow. They change a number of times until they finally grow into a star shape. This process of

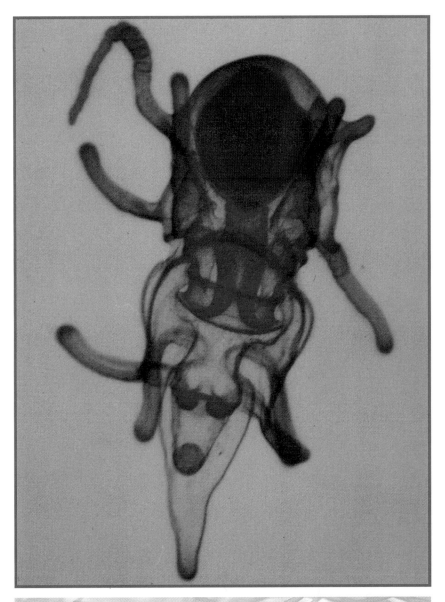

The larva of a sea star looks nothing like the adult.

changing is called a *metamorphosis,* and it is as complicated as the metamorphosis of a butterfly.

A few kinds of sea stars "hatch" their young, similar to the way sea horses do. Instead of letting the eggs float freely in the water, these sea stars carry their eggs near their mouth until they hatch into tiny sea stars. There is no larval stage.

Sea stars reproduce in yet another way. In some cases, the center disk of a sea star may divide into halves. Each half grows its missing parts and becomes a

new sea star. Or in some cases, a sea star can simply cast off an arm, and the arm will form a new disc and the other missing arms. The arms of most sea stars, however, die if they are separated from the disk.

Different kinds of sea stars live for different lengths of time. Usually sea stars live from five to twenty years. Sea star *fossils*, the remains of sea stars from a long time ago, show that the sea star has not changed much through the passing of millions of years.

Dead sea stars can be dried to reveal their skeletons.

The ochre star is not always yellow as its name suggests.

5

Stars of Every Stripe and Color

⭐

Not all sea stars look alike. The common sea star of the Pacific Coast is the ochre star. It grows to between 6 and 14 inches (15 and 36 cm) across. It is brown, yellow, or purple.

The sea bat has very blunt arms. It gets its name from the fact that the blunt rays look almost like bat wings. It is red, yellow, or purple and measures about 7 inches (18 cm) across. It is found in tide pools and in the deep water of the Pacific Coast.

The purple sea star is one of those that forms its body into a hump, puts out its tube feet, and pulls oysters apart. Purple sea stars are found along the northeast coast of the United States. They are colored blue, pink, rose, and red, and they measure from 6 to 17 inches (15 to 43 cm) across.

The common sun star is especially beautiful. It has from eight to fourteen arms. The center of this sea star is a bright red. Its arms have colored bands of pink and white. Like the purple sea star, it is fond of eating oysters. It grows from 14 to 20 inches (36 to 51 cm) from the tip of one arm to the tip of another. Common sun stars are found on both the Atlantic and Pacific coasts of the United States.

The mud-star is a small sea star. It is only 3 or 4 inches (8 to 10 cm) across. The slender-armed sea star is also small, measuring from 2 to 4 inches (5 to 10 cm) across. The slender-armed sea star is either a light purple or a pale pink. This tiny sea star is one of those that carry young in a brood *sac* near its mouth until the eggs have hatched and the little sea stars have grown.

The blood sea star also makes a kind of pouch near its mouth where it keeps its eggs. This sea star is between 2 and 4 inches (5 to 10 cm) across. Usually it is a rich red, orange, purple, or rose. Sometimes it is a cream color. Most sea stars have four rows of tube feet, but the blood sea star has only two rows of tube feet.

The purple sun star is often called the eleven armed sun star, but it may have anywhere from seven to thirteen arms, or rays. Most often it has nine or ten arms. It is purple with a gold margin around it. This sea star grows to be more than 16 inches (41 cm) across.

*The morning sun star may have as
many as fourteen rays.*

A pincushion sea star is shaped like a pentagon.

One kind of sea stars found along the coast of South America looks like a giant sunflower. It has up to forty-four arms. Other sunflower stars are found along the coast from Alaska to Southern California. These big sunflower stars grow to be 2 feet (60 cm) or more across. They may have up to twenty-four arms.

Still others, such as the cushion stars, have almost no arms at all. They look more like a *pentagon* than a star.

Brittle stars are another kind of sea star. Their arms are sharply marked off from the center. As their name suggests, brittle stars easily lose their arms and grow new ones. These sea stars can move faster than most because their arms make a snakelike motion to crawl across the sand.

Like the common sea star, eggs of brittle stars hatch into tiny, swimming animals. These change into small brittle stars. It takes two or three years for them to reach full size. Brittle stars eat small sea animals such as worms.

The green brittle star is hard to spot even though it lives in shallow water. Its color helps it hide behind plants.

The daisy brittle star has banded arms. It is sometimes colored red and white and sometimes green and brown. The daisy brittle star has a 1-inch (3-cm) body with arms that grow about 3 inches (8 cm) long. It is found on both the Atlantic and Pacific coasts.

Then there are the serpent stars. The long-armed snake-star has arms like threads that are only about 1 1/2 inches (4 cm) long. This snake-star is grayish-white or pale blue. It lives along the northeastern coast of the United States.

One of the strangest looking of all these little animals is the basket star. It has five branching arms that

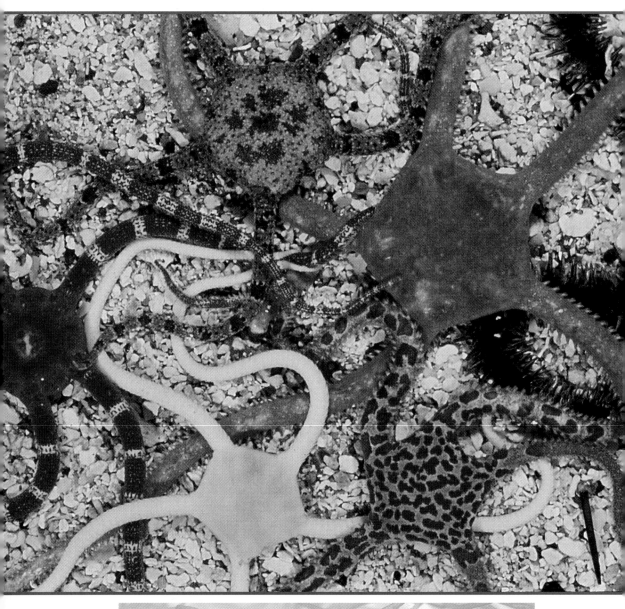

Brittle stars have snakelike arms that break off easily.

grow to be 9 to 14 inches (23 to 36 cm) long. Sometimes groups of these basket stars tangle together and make a sort of net for catching tiny floating plankton to eat. The basket star has a star-shaped mouth with five jaws. It can coil around rocks or seaweed.

So you see, stars are found not only in the sky, and dragons do not live just in storybooks. One day you may discover for yourself the living stars and dragons of the sea.

If you are fortunate enough to live on or visit a coast, you can see these creatures in their natural setting. Otherwise, you can study them in aquariums. Either way, you will learn that sea stars and dragons are indeed strange and magical.

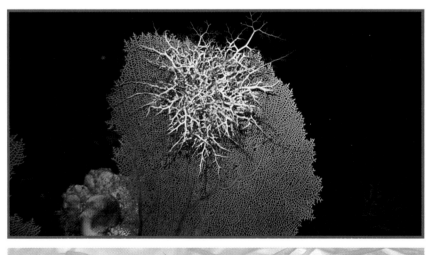

A group of basket stars make a net on a blue sea fan.

≈ *Glossary* ≈

anemone—a sea animal that looks like a flower.

brood pouch—the pocket on the front of a male sea horse where eggs are kept until they hatch.

camouflage—means of disguise or concealment.

cirri—slender body parts attached to an animal, such as the "whiskers" on a sea horse.

corals—colonies of animals called polyps that live together with the skeletal material they secrete.

dorsal fin—the fin on the back of a fish.

fossil—the remains or impression of an animal from millions of years ago.

gills—organs for obtaining oxygen from the water.

marine—having to do with the sea or the ocean.

metamorphosis—a change of form or structure that an animal, such as a butterfly or a sea star, goes through as it grows up.

mussel—a sea animal that has a long shell.

pentagon—a shape with five equal sides.

plankton—animals and plants too tiny to see that live in bodies of water.

ray—the arm of a sea star.

regeneration—the ability to grow new body parts to replace parts that have been torn off.

sac—a baglike part of an animal.

scallop—a sea animal that has a shell with wavy edges.

spawn—to produce eggs as fish do.

For Further Reading

Ancona, George. *The Aquarium Book*. New York: Clarion Books, 1991.

Clark, John. *Seas and Oceans*. New York: Gloucester Press, 1992.

Coldrey, Jennifer. *Life in the Sea*. New York: Bookwright Press, 1991.

Cooper, Jason. *Small Sea Creatures*. Vero Beach, FL: Rourke Corp., 1992.

Curtis, Patricia. *Aquatic Animals in the Wild and in Captivity*. New York: Dutton, 1992.

Fowler, Allan. *It Could Still Be a Fish*. Chicago: Childrens Press, 1990.

Rice, Tony. *Ocean World*. Brookfield, CT: Millbrook Press, 1991.

Rood, Ronald N. *Tide Pools.* New York: HarperCollins, 1993.

Royston, Angela. *Sea Animals.* New York: Aladdin Books, 1992.

Taylor, Barbara. *Coral Reef.* New York: Dorling Kindersley, 1992.

Twist, Clint. *Seas and Oceans.* New York: Dillon Press, 1991.

Wu, Norbert. *Life in the Oceans.* Boston: Little, Brown, 1991.

≈ *Index* ≈

62

≈ About ≈ the Author

Phyllis J. Perry has written two dozen books for teachers and young people. Her latest book for Watts is *The Fiddlehoppers: Crickets, Katydids, and Locusts.* She has a bachelor degree from the University of California, Berkeley, and a doctorate from the University of Colorado. Dr. Perry lives with her husband, David, in Boulder, Colorado, where they spend lots of time in the mountains. But they make a point of visiting both coasts often to walk along the beach and make discoveries about life in the sea.